The Journey to Freedom

Bethany World Prayer Center
13855 Plank Road • Baker, Louisiana 70714
Phone: (225) 774-1700 • Fax: (225) 774-2335
Web site: www.bethany.com or www.bccn.com

D1219195

Copyright © 2005 by Bethany World Prayer Center

The Journey to Freedom: An Encounter With God
by the Staff of Bethany World Prayer Center

Printed in the United States of America

ISBN-10: 0-9727659-4-8
ISBN-13: 978-0-9727659-4-7

Contents

Introduction

Welcome to the journey of your life! When you found Christ, you began a wonderful journey of discovery and adventure. Giving your life to Him thrust you down the pathway to freedom in body, mind, and soul. Your life has taken on an entirely new dimension because of the decision you made to follow Christ.

This book is designed to help you as you begin the journey of your new life in Christ. Because the cross of Christ is so central to the Christian faith, we have chosen it as the unifying theme for these first ninety days of your journey. We are going to take you *to the cross* by preparing you for a life-changing Encounter Retreat. Then we will take you *through the cross* as we bring you to the weekend retreat. Finally, we will teach you how to continue your journey *with the cross* as we show you how to maintain the freedom you'll find at the Encounter Retreat.

The book is divided into three sections: preparation for an Encounter Retreat, the actual Encounter Retreat, and follow-up after the retreat. Each section is vital to your Christian journey, so don't miss any of it! Commit yourself to these ninety days of change, and watch what God will do in you. You will be amazed, and you will never be the same again. So join us now, and *let the journey begin!*

The JOURNEY to FREEDOM

The Journey to the Cross

An *Encounter* with God

Lesson 1
A Great Decision
The Journey Out of Egypt

Here are the stages in the journey of the Israelites when they came out of Egypt by divisions under the leadership of Moses and Aaron.

—Numbers 33:1

You have just made a great decision! You may have attended a church service where you responded to a call to come to the altar and receive Christ, or you may have attended a home cell group meeting and met Christ there. Perhaps a friend prayed with you to receive Christ. However you came to this decision, it was the right one! The decision to follow Christ is the greatest and most life-changing decision that you will ever make.

The decision to follow Christ starts you on a journey that lasts a lifetime. But you have taken the first step, and from this point on, you're entering a new way of living and a new way of looking at things. You're leaving the past behind, and you're moving toward a future bright with hope and promise.

Your journey is remarkably similar to another journey spoken of in the Bible: the journey of God's people from Egypt to the Promised Land. For many years, the people of Israel lived in Egypt, having gone there in a time of famine. As time passed, their numbers increased greatly, and the Egyptian rulers became concerned about their loyalty. Thus began a number of years of oppression for God's people in Egypt. Finally, God raised up a deliverer, Moses, who led the Israelites out of Egypt, free from the terrible oppression of Pharaoh.

This is a picture of what happened to you when you came to Christ. You left the "Egypt" of sin, oppression, and despair, and you began a journey to the Promised Land. You were delivered and set free from the grasp of sin. No longer were you a slave of "Pharaoh," but you became a beloved child of God Most High. Just like the Israelites, you will walk through various stages in your journey, but you've already taken the most important step. Let's see what this first step, your decision to come to Christ, means.

What does it all mean?

Do you understand where you stood before you decided to follow Christ and where you stand today after having made this decision? Things have now changed! God sees you differently, and you probably see God differently. Let's think about what has happened to you: "But God demonstrates His own love for us in this: While we were still sinners, Christ died for us" (Rom. 5:8).

You were a sinner!

Being a sinner means that you had failed to do what God required of you in order to be in right relationship with Him. In other words, you had failed to fulfill God's law, just like all of us: "For all have sinned and fall short of the glory of God" (Rom. 3:23). Sin includes those things you do that are not acceptable to God, as well as your natural tendency to walk in disobedience to God.

As a sinner, you could not please God.

"As it is written: 'There is no one righteous, not even one; there is no one who understands, no one who seeks God. All have turned away; they have together become worthless; there is no one who does good, not one'" (Rom. 3:10). Most of us live our lives without ever considering what God might expect from us. But you probably discovered that even when you tried to live right and please God, you couldn't. That's because without Christ it is impossible.

You see, you were dead in your sin!

Even though God loved you, you were separated from Him. Because God is totally good and perfect, He cannot allow sin in His presence. So until you met Christ, you were not able to enter into God's presence. But now, because of His shed blood, Christ has become your passage to the Father.

Ephesians 2:2 says that you formerly "followed the ways of this world." In the past, you lived for the world and its attractions—under the direct influence of Satan. The spirit of rebellion controlled your life through strong desires of lust and greed. This spirit cannot and will not ever gain God's approval. So every person under this influence must come to Christ. That's where you were, until you met Christ!

Because God loves you so much . . .

He still dealt with your heart through the influence of the Holy Spirit, no matter how hardhearted you became. Something probably happened to you that left you desperate, empty, and in need of God, and He was there to draw you to Himself by inviting you to know His Son, Jesus.

If you had refused God's love . . .

If you had refused to accept God's love and offer of eternal life through Jesus Christ, then you would have remained in your sin and continued to be separated from God. If you had died separated from God, you would have been condemned to an eternity without God in a place the Bible calls "hell."

Ephesians 2:1–3 says, "As for you, you were dead in your transgressions and sins, in which you used to live when you followed the ways of this world and of the ruler of the kingdom of the air, the spirit who is now at work in those who are disobedient. All of us also lived among them at one time, gratifying the cravings of our sinful nature and following its desires and thoughts. Like the rest, we were by nature objects of wrath."

What did it mean when you got saved?

Good question! We often see people performing religious duties with the hope of gaining God's approval. We have already discovered, however, that just doing good things cannot please God. By itself, the act of responding to the altar call after a sermon can't save you either.

If you didn't earn it, and the preacher didn't save you, what really happened?

Another great question! Let's look at God's clear answer: "For it is by grace you have been saved, through faith—and this is not from yourselves, it is the gift of God—not by works, so that no one can boast" (Eph. 2:8–9). You were saved by grace—favor that God gave you. It was undeserved, unearned, and given freely. Grace came to you through faith, and faith means being totally convinced that something is true. In this case, it means having the assurance that Christ paid for your sins.

When you firmly believed that it was through Christ alone that you could have salvation (not by anything you could do), you experienced "saving faith." Before you had this faith, you had no grace or favor with God. Ephesians 2:12 says, "Remember that at that time you were separate from Christ . . . without hope and without God in the world."

Because of your faith in Christ, you now have grace and are in God's favor! Now you can enter God's presence boldly, knowing that you have received mercy and forgiveness. God accepts you now through the work of Christ.

Now what is expected of you?

The Bible has a very good answer to that question. Ephesians 4:1–3 says, "As a prisoner for the Lord, then, I urge you to live a life worthy of the calling you have received. Be completely humble and gentle; be

patient, bearing with one another in love. Make every effort to keep the unity of the Spirit through the bond of peace."

With God's help through the power of the Holy Spirit, you are expected to "live a life worthy" of God's salvation, reflecting your new relationship with God. Your new life should be different from your old life. As you walk with Christ, you will learn humility, love, patience, and many other virtues (positive Christlike attitudes) that will help you to please God. As you are learning these virtues and walking in unity with other Christians, you will continue to have confidence that you are a child of God.

Discussion Questions

1.   How did God see your life before your decision to receive Christ?

2.   What did you do to become a Christian?

3.   What one thing caused you to see your need for Christ?

4.   How has your life changed since receiving Christ?

5.   If you died right now, would you go to heaven? Why?

Lesson 2
The Power of the Cross
The Journey to the Promised Land

Take possession of the land and settle in it, for I have given you the land to possess.

—Numbers 33:53

When the Israelites left Egypt, they were headed to a land especially prepared for them. This Promised Land was a wonderful place, full of blessing and prosperity. But in order to enjoy it with all its benefits, the Israelites had to actually walk in and possess it.

It's the same way for you in this new journey you've begun. You've left Egypt, but you're going to have to walk into your Promised Land. God has so much waiting for you and He wants to give it to you, but you're going to have to possess it, just like the Israelites had to do.

When you made your commitment to Christ, you became the beneficiary of all the rights and privileges that He won for you by His death on the cross. This is the Promised Land of your Christian faith. When you became His child, you became an heir to heaven and all its riches. Romans 8:17 says it like this: "Now if we are children, then we are heirs—heirs of God and co-heirs with Christ."

If you are an heir to an earthly inheritance, your inheritance is spelled out in a will that goes into effect only upon the death of the person who made it. Similarly, when Christ died on the cross, all the riches of heaven were now made available to you as His heir (Heb. 9:15–17). Because He died, you can have eternal

life. Because He suffered, you can have physical healing. Because He was wounded, you can be made whole. By looking at what happened to Jesus on the cross, you can get a better picture of what He bought for you as an heir of heaven.

When Jesus died on the cross, Hebrews 10:20 says that "a new and living way [was] opened for us through the curtain, that is, his body." In other words, the battered, bruised, and torn flesh of Christ was a door into a breakthrough. Every place where His flesh was "broken through" symbolizes a "new and living way" into the Promised Land of freedom and deliverance never before guaranteed. We can group these breakthroughs that Jesus won for you into four main areas: healing for your body, peace for your mind, cleansing for your conscience, and healing for your heart (spirit).

A breakthrough in your body: the whip

Isaiah 53:5 is perhaps one of the most frequently quoted verses in the Old Testament. The last part of that verse, "By His stripes we are healed" (NKJV), talks of the physical wounds inflicted on Jesus' body. The first tear in His flesh came with the scourging ordered by Pilate (Matt. 27:26). In scourging, the Roman legionnaire took a whip that had lead balls tied to each strand. The victim was then tied and beaten a maximum of thirty-nine lashes with this horrible instrument. The punishment was so brutal that many people did not survive it.

Because Jesus endured this agonizing flogging, the price was paid for your physical healing. From the back of Christ flowed the blood for the healing of your body from every disease, affliction, or condition. Peter expressed this thought in 1 Peter 2:24: "He himself bore our sins in his body on the tree, so that we might die to sins and live for righteousness; by his wounds you have been healed." Sickness was paid for on the cross, and as an heir with Christ, you have the right to walk through that open door and receive the inheritance of healing.

A breakthrough in your mind: the crown of thorns

In the events leading up to the actual crucifixion, the Roman soldiers placed a crown of thorns upon the precious head of Jesus (Matt. 27:29), thrusting it deep into his scalp. This crown of thorns represents the "punishment that brought us peace" (Isa. 53:5).

Christ wore the crown of thorns to bring breakthrough in the area of your mind. Just like thorns are the fruit of a branch, your mind bears the sinful fruit of worry, anxiety, pride, depression, lust, and greed. But when Christ willingly wore that awful crown, He was taking God's judgment upon every rebellious, renegade thought that you would ever have. Because He bore this judgment, no evil thought can control you, and you don't have to be the victim of ungodly, sinful thought patterns anymore.

In 2 Corinthians 10:5 KJV, the Bible speaks of "casting down imaginations, and every high thing that exalteth itself against the knowledge of God, and bringing into captivity every thought to the obedience of Christ." In other words, you can "capture" every thought and make it line up with the Word of God, because of what Jesus has already done for you. Every thought has been conquered by the blood that flowed from the head of Christ. As a child of God and a heavenly heir, you can have victory over thoughts of fear, worry, depression, addiction, or any mental struggle.

A breakthrough in your conscience: the nails

Each of us has a long list, or record, of our failures, weaknesses, and shortcomings. These can be called "transgressions." However, again in Isaiah 53:5, the Bible says that "he was pierced for our transgressions." Isaiah perceived a connection between Jesus' being pierced (the opening of the holes where He was nailed) and our transgressions.

Between Christ's hands and the cross was the list of your sins, symbolically. When the nails went through His hands, they also pierced the list that was between His hands and the wood of the cross. Colossians 2:14

NLT says, "He canceled the record that contained the charges against us. He took it and destroyed it by nailing it to Christ's cross." So each and every sin of your past has been paid for. The record of your transgressions has been canceled! Your sins were like a certificate of debt that has now been marked "paid in full" because of what Christ endured on the cross. You don't have to feel guilty and condemned for your sins, because the nail-scarred hands of Jesus bore your guilt so you could go free. You can lay your head upon your pillow each night and go to sleep with a clear conscience.

A breakthrough in your heart (spirit): the spear

Back in Isaiah 53:5, the Bible says that Jesus was "crushed for our iniquities." Christ's heart was crushed and broken by the weight of iniquity that He carried for all humanity.

After Jesus finally succumbed, a soldier pierced His side with a spear, and there was "a sudden flow of blood and water" (John 19:34). From a medical standpoint, this indicates that Jesus' heart had ruptured and that blood had filled His heart. After He died, the serum separated from the coagulated blood in His heart. As a result, the opening of His side produced a stream of water and an oozing of coagulated blood.

Christ died of a broken heart, literally. His heart was broken that yours might be healed. Inside the broken heart of Christ is a world of freedom, healing, and reconciliation. It is yours as a joint-heir of Christ, if you'll receive it.

The death of Christ on the hill of Calvary was the pivotal point of all history. It marked the point from which all humanity could receive forgiveness of sins and total healing of body, mind, and spirit. As awful as it seemed at the time, it was yet the most triumphant act of all time. The Son of God defeated death, destruction, and the devil and opened the gates of heaven for all eternity.

As a child of God, you have a wonderful divine inheritance. Physical healing, emotional health, a clear conscience, and a mended heart are all yours as an heir of heaven. Look to the cross each day of your life and thank God anew for what Jesus suffered for you. Look to the cross and see the great love He has for you. Look to the cross and be healed—body, mind, and spirit. Look to the cross and be set free!

Discussion Questions

1. In what four areas did Christ win a breakthrough for you when He died on the cross?

2. In which of these areas do you need to see the power of the cross at work in your life?

3. Spend some time discussing the benefits of the cross with your teacher or cell leader.

Lesson 3
Water Baptism and Deliverance
The Journey Out of Bondage

They journeyed from before Hahiroth and passed through the midst of the sea.

—Numbers 33:8 NASB

In the last chapter, you studied the cross and how the blood of Jesus, the spotless Lamb of God, sets you free from sin, sickness, and bondage. First Corinthians 5:7 refers to Christ as the Passover Lamb, the one who was slain on our behalf. This is actually referring to Jesus' fulfillment of something that happened to God's people in the Old Testament as they were leaving the bondage of Egypt.

When God raised up Moses to lead the Israelites out of Egypt, Moses presented a series of petitions to Pharaoh to let God's people go. Hardened of heart, Pharaoh resisted, and a series of plagues and calamities befell the land, culminating with the event that came to be known as the Passover. On that fateful night, an angel of death struck down every firstborn son of the Egyptians, but "passed over" the homes of the Israelites who had applied the blood of a spotless lamb to their doorposts.

Although Pharaoh relented and let the people go, this was not the end of their journey. In fact, it was just beginning, as they did not enter into the Promised Land for forty more years! It's the same for you, too. When you come to Christ, you are just beginning your journey. You have not yet entered into all the blessings that are waiting for you in your spiritual Promised Land. You know what's available there through the power of the cross, but you still have a lot to learn before you actually get there.

Leaving Egypt and entering the Promised Land

You may be out of Egypt, but Egypt may not be out of you!

Pharaoh did not give up just because the people left Egypt. He could not stand the thought that he had lost millions of slaves. So he decided to go after them. That's just like the devil does with you! He can't stand the idea that you are now free from his power. He will do everything he can to try to drag you back to "Egypt." He doesn't want you free and victorious in Christ. He'll try to get you to always look back and long for the "good old days" instead of keeping your focus on the journey ahead and the future God has planned for you.

Pharaoh had a plan to enslave the Israelites again, but God had an even bigger one. His plan was so great and so awesome that the world has never forgotten it. It's a story that you probably heard as a child: the journey through the Red Sea. Let's look at this story and see what it means for you.

You need to cross through the Red Sea!

God told Moses and all Israel to camp by the Red Sea until Pharaoh came very close with all his troops (Ex. 14:1–4). The people did as instructed, and soon Pharaoh was upon them. That night, Moses stretched his rod over the sea, and the sea miraculously opened. The three million people of Israel crossed under cover of darkness (vv. 21–22).

Seeing the sea open, Pharaoh's army decided to pursue. At just the right moment, Moses stretched out his rod and the sea completely buried all of Pharaoh's horses and charioteers. The people rejoiced on the shore of the Red Sea because not only had they escaped their enemy, but now their enemy had been totally defeated!

God wants you to be free indeed, separated from "Egypt," or the world, so that it has no more power over your life. But even after having the blood of the Passover Lamb applied to your heart and beginning the journey of leaving Egypt, you're going to have to walk through the Red Sea. There's no other way to get to the Promised Land God has waiting for you.

The Red Sea means two very important things in your life. First, the Red Sea (a body of water) is a picture of water baptism. Just as "they were all baptized into Moses in the cloud and in the sea" (1 Cor. 10:2), you need to be baptized at the beginning of your Christian journey. Water baptism is, therefore, quite necessary—not for your salvation (the blood of the Lamb did that), but for your freedom.

Second, the Red Sea symbolizes deliverance. Not until the Israelites walked through the sea were they free from Egypt's power. When you came to Christ, your old habits, thoughts, and bondages were crushed by God's power, but you, like Israel, are going to have to learn how to walk in that freedom.

Let's look at these two aspects, water baptism and deliverance, in a little more detail.

The power of water baptism

Baptism is like a burial of your old life (Rom. 6:3–4).

As God's people walked through the Red Sea, the wall of water was so high on either side of them that they appeared to go down into the water and disappear. When you are water baptized, you are immersed into the water, just like Jesus was when John baptized Him in the Jordan River (Mark 1:9–10).

This "going down" into the water is like a burial. It symbolizes that your old life has ended (in Egypt) and that you are starting a brand new life (without Pharaoh). Paul said that we are "buried with Him through baptism into death, so that as Christ was raised from the dead through the glory of the Father, so we too might walk in newness of life" (Rom. 6:4 NASB).

Baptism is important for your conscience (Heb. 10:22).

Your conscience is that part of your soul that either assures you or condemns you about your past. Water baptism is "an appeal to God for a good conscience" (1 Pet. 3:21 NASB). Your conscience needs to feel clean, like it has had a bath, and that's what water baptism does for you. It's a point in time when you publicly declare that you have buried the past and are moving on in your journey with the Lord.

Hebrews 10:22 NASB says, "Let us draw near with a sincere heart in full assurance of faith, having our hearts sprinkled clean from an evil conscience and our bodies washed with pure water." This is just what water baptism does for you!

The power of deliverance

Pharaoh had an army, and so does Satan!

Satan has an army of demonic powers that are highly skilled at manifesting their personalities through human beings. One man that Christ set free had a legion, or as many as 6,000, demon spirits inside his body (Mark 5:9)! By the blood of Jesus, Satan's power has been broken over your life. However, he will still seek to control your body, mind, and heart. He will try to keep you bound up with bad habits and addictions. He will attack your thoughts and emotions. And he will especially try to keep you in the grip of bitterness and unforgiveness. All his intentions for you are evil, because there is nothing good in him.

Paul said, "Do not give the devil a foothold" (Eph. 4:27). Even though you are saved, there may be areas in your life that are grieving the Holy Spirit and giving Satan a legal foothold in which he can freely operate. That's why we are preparing you for a wonderful weekend retreat where you can deal with these issues. As part of that weekend, you are going to experience the mighty power of God to deliver you and set you free from all those things.

Deliverance is a spiritual housecleaning.

Jesus told us that when an unclean spirit leaves a person, it seeks to return: " 'I will return to the house I left.' When it arrives, it finds the house unoccupied, swept clean and put in order" (Matt. 12:44). When you get saved, your spirit is now "swept clean," free of the dirt and stain of sin. However, if you don't do a thorough "housecleaning" and let the Holy Spirit "occupy" you, Satan will be able to return: "Then it goes and takes with it seven other spirits more wicked than itself, and they go in and live there. And the final condition of that man is worse than the first" (Matt. 12:45).

This is why many new Christians do not stay free. They have not completely renounced and removed Satan as an illegal resident in their body, mind, and spirit. They have left him as an occupant instead of forcefully evicting him!

How Satan seeks to retain control

There are three main ways Satan seeks to retain control in your life, even after you come to Christ. First are *generational bondages* (Ex. 20:5). These are patterns of addiction, habits, criminal activity, divorce, and other such things that have moved through your family line, perhaps for decades. Through the blood of Christ, you have been set free from these things, but you need to enforce that freedom by renouncing the power of those generational bondages.

Curses (Gal. 3:13–14) are a second way in which Satan tries to control you. God told Israel that if they broke the Law, a curse would come upon them in their finances, their emotions, their health, their mental health, and in other areas (Deut. 28). When you live in violation of God's Word, Satan has a legal right to enforce the curse of the Law. When you come to Christ, however, the curse is broken, paid for by the blood of Jesus. As Proverbs 26:2 says, "Like a fluttering sparrow or a darting swallow, an undeserved curse does not come to rest."

Soul ties are a third tactic Satan uses against you. A soul tie is an unspiritual connection between you and someone else that you have a deep (often sexual) relationship with. That unholy relationship gives Satan access and is an open door into your life. God forbade Israel to maintain those kinds of relationships: "But if you do not drive out the inhabitants of the land from before you, then it shall come about that those whom you let remain of them will become as pricks in your eyes and as thorns in your sides, and they will trouble you in the land in which you live" (Num. 33:55 NASB).

Breaking Satan's strongholds

Bondages, curses, and soul ties have all been broken by the blood of Jesus on the cross. However, *you* must declare your total freedom from destructive habits, addictions, emotions, thoughts, and relationships. This is part of the total housecleaning you'll do on the Encounter Retreat so that Satan has no more access into your life.

Begin preparing yourself now for this next step in your personal journey with Christ. *Renounce* Satan with your mouth in any of those areas where he is trying to control you, and *pronounce* your freedom. Forgive and release all those who have contributed to your bondage in the past. And finally, *rejoice* in your liberty, like Israel did on the Red Sea shore after their mighty deliverance (Ex. 15:20).

Your old enemies have been defeated, and you are about to journey to a personal three-day encounter with God. You are leaving Egypt behind forever and walking through the Red Sea of deliverance. You are headed straight for the Promised Land as you continue the journey to the cross.

An *Encounter* with God

Discussion Questions

1. Why is water baptism necessary? Have you taken this important step? If not, make arrangements to do so.

2. How is water baptism like a burial and resurrection? How does this apply to your life?

3. What are the three main ways Satan seeks to retain control in your life?

4. How can you break the power of Satan over your life?

Lesson 4
Encountering God
The Journey to the Cross

You are now to the point in your journey with Christ where you are ready to encounter God in a very special way. You have made a decision to follow Him, you have learned what Jesus did on the cross, you have taken the important step of being water-baptized, and you have learned about deliverance. Now it's time to prepare yourself for a life-changing experience called the Encounter Retreat.

What is an Encounter?

An Encounter is a divine appointment with God. It is a specific time in your life when God "shows up" on your behalf. It is marked by His presence, His power, and His deliverance. When you encounter God, you are forever changed by the experience.

The Scriptures abound with many instances of individuals who had their own special encounters with God. Consider Jacob, who after wrestling with the angel at Peniel said, "I have seen God face to face" (Gen. 32:30 KJV). After that experience, Jacob's name was changed, noting the transforming power of his encounter, and always thereafter he walked with a limp as a reminder of the night he wrestled with the angel of the Lord. In the New Testament, person after person was radically changed as each came into contact with Jesus. Because of encountering Him, sick bodies were healed, tormented minds were set free, blind eyes were opened, and even the dead were raised to life. There is truly no end to what can happen when a person encounters God.

Although God is the one who initiates the encounter, deciding the when, where, and how of it, you have an important part to play in the process. Your role is to make yourself available to God and to be willing to cooperate with Him in whatever He wishes to do in your life. Your attitude must be one of surrender, acknowledging Him as the potter who has the right to do with you whatever He chooses. If you will entrust yourself to Him, take the step of going on an Encounter, and maintain an open heart, you will have your own uniquely special experience with God. And just like all the people in the Bible, you will never be the same!

What practical preparations should you make to get ready for your Encounter Retreat weekend?

In the days preceding your Encounter, you will, of course, take care of those ordinary things that we all have to deal with. You will want to make sure that you leave your family on the right note. Leave your home in order, with all details taken care of. It is important that family members understand where you are going and why and are prepared to take care of themselves in your absence.

Ladies, see that your children will have proper supervision while you are gone. Clean the house and do the laundry. Make sure your husband and children have something to eat. You want to do whatever you can to make it easy for them while you are gone. Husbands, if you are the one going on the Encounter, leave your home in order, too. Fill the car with gas, mow the grass, and tend to those little things that you've been meaning to get around to. The main idea is to leave home on a good note, with no room for the devil to plant a seed of resentment in your loved ones because you did not provide for them before leaving.

Most importantly, do not leave home angry with a family member. Resolve any problems before going on your Encounter so that you will be free to concentrate on what the Lord wants to do in you. You want to do everything within your power to make sure that you arrive at the retreat center free of worry, anxiety, or unresolved issues concerning your family.

Another point to make here deals with your employment. Make all arrangements at work sufficiently in advance. If you need to leave early, get permission. Be honest and upfront with your employer about where you are going and why. Most people are happy to work with you. If you have a difficult employer, don't yield to the temptation to use deceit or manipulation to get what you want. Trust God to make a way for you at the right time in the right way as you conduct yourself in the right manner.

How do you prepare yourself spiritually for the Encounter?

Even more important than the physical preparations you make are the spiritual ones necessary to ensure that you have a good Encounter. The most important thing you can do to get yourself ready is to consciously develop an attitude of openness and transparency before the Lord. In the days leading up to the Encounter, make a deliberate step of surrender to the Lord and whatever He wants to do. Ask the Holy Spirit to remove preconceived ideas from your mind and to enable you to go as an empty vessel waiting to be filled. Allow the Lord to stir up an expectancy in you that you will indeed encounter Him on your weekend.

Many things will pull at you and try to distract you from your purpose, but decide ahead of time that nothing will stop you from having your encounter with God. Listed below are a few of the things that you might need to deal with to prepare yourself spiritually for the Encounter:

- **Personal relationships**—Sometimes those we love most, such as our families and friends, are our greatest hindrance in following God. You must determine to follow your Savior, no matter what (Matt. 16:24–25). You must give Him free rein to change you and mold you into His image without worrying about what others will think of you. You must put Him first, before all others (Mark 3:31–35; 10:29–30). When you go on your Encounter, therefore, lay aside all thoughts of those you are leaving at home. If you bring the problems of home or relationships with you into your Encounter, you will be distracted from what God wants to do in you.

- **Personal plans and ambition**—Are you going on this Encounter with an agenda of your own? Do you want God to work in your life, but only in certain areas and ways? Are you trying to dictate to God what to do and how to do it? To truly encounter the Lord, you must lay aside preconceived ideas of what God may or may not do. You have to die to yourself (John 12:24) and be open and transparent before Him. If you will do this, God will move in powerfully and accomplish the work He wants to do.

- **Personal possessions**—The things you own can mean too much to you. Every good thing you have was given to you by God (James 1:17), and He is more than able to take care of your things while you are away on an Encounter. The Word of God is clear. If you seek Him and His kingdom, He will take care of you and provide for your needs (Matt. 6:33). Nothing is so valuable as to be of more worth than encountering the living God.

What will you experience on the Encounter?

The effects of an Encounter are many and varied, depending on what God specifically does in your heart. You may experience a freedom that you've never known before, a new confidence in God's love for you, a fresh infilling of the Holy Spirit, and boundless joy in the goodness of God. But whatever happens, we find that, in particular, many people experience the following changes:

- **Repentance (Ps. 51:3–4)**—At the Encounter, most people will come face to face with their own sinfulness and need for forgiveness. All of us have sinned and need to periodically examine our hearts for any areas that are not pleasing to God. The Encounter provides the perfect time and place to get right with God in any way you need to. The repentance will be characterized by a change in life and attitude, not just by sorrow or emotional feelings of regret.

- **New direction (Matt. 4:18–20)**—When Peter and Andrew, ordinary fishermen, encountered Jesus, their lives took a drastic new direction. They left behind all the old and familiar and launched out into

the deep waters of following the Lord. It can be the same for you. The Encounter is an opportunity for you to start on a new course, no matter what your past has been like.

- **Transformed character (Gen. 32:1–8, 27–28)**—When Jacob had an encounter with the Lord, his relationship with his brother Esau changed. Even his very name changed. You will be forever changed in your innermost being if you will allow the Lord to have His way with you at the Encounter.

- **Renewed love (John 21:14–19)**—In the New Testament, Peter boldly declared that he was willing to follow the Lord, even to death, but as the story unfolds, we read how He denied the Lord three times. Then after Jesus' resurrection, Peter was restored and given a place of authority. He was given a second chance to prove Himself, and prove Himself he did as mightily evidenced in the book of Acts. God will give you a second chance, too. If you let Him have His way with you on the Encounter, you will find yourself falling in love with Him all over again, and you will be able to walk with the fire of your "first love" into the new path He has for you.

Your Encounter weekend is a weekend like no other. It is a landmark event in your Christian journey. As you grow in God, you will look back on that event as a turning point in your life. At the Encounter, you will come face to face with Christ at the cross. At the cross, you will find forgiveness, joy, and a new reason for living. Let's embark on this journey together, and let's get ready to encounter God!

Discussion Questions

1.   Why is it so important for everyone to go on an Encounter?

2.   Name someone from the Bible who encountered God, and describe his experience.

3.   What change do you hope to experience on your Encounter?

4.   What steps will you take to get ready for your Encounter?

The JOURNEY to FREEDOM

The Journey Through the Cross

An Encounter with God

The Encounter Retreat

Congratulations on your decision to continue your journey with Christ on this very special weekend. Thank you for taking the time and making the effort to be here. You will be glad you did!

An Encounter Retreat is a dramatic experience that can completely change the course of your life. You have already experienced many important milestones, or encounters, in your life: falling in love and getting married, being accepted into a university, obtaining a job, or any other number of important events. But of all the encounters you could have, the most important one of all is an encounter with the living God!

The Encounter Retreat brings you face to face with the cross of Christ and what it means to your life. Through a series of experiences and personal teachings, you'll see visible, manifested change in your life. In this safe, confidential environment, you'll learn how to establish your relationship with God, how to have direct fellowship with Him, and how to commit to His lordship. The claims of the Gospel and their relevance to you will be explained, and you'll experience forgiveness of sin, deliverance from bondage, emotional and physical healing, and restoration of worth and value.

The Bible gives us many examples of people who were radically transformed by their personal encounters with the Lord Jesus. Remember the stories of the Samaritan woman (John 4:5–29), Zacchaeus (Luke 19:1–10), the Gadarene demoniac (Matt. 8:28–34), and all the disciples of Christ. After these people had an encounter with the Lord Jesus, they were never the same again. You can be assured that when you, too, have an encounter with Him, you will never be the same.

This weekend, why not seize the opportunity to experience God? Go a little further on the journey you've begun and visit the cross in all its power. Walk right up to the cross of Calvary, receive its forgiveness, and walk through it to your Promised Land of victory, joy, and peace. Are you ready for this powerful, exciting phase of your journey? Let's begin it *now!*

Note-taking space for 13 sessions has been provided on the following pages.
Use as many as are applicable to your particular retreat.

Title: _____

Notes:_____

_____

_____

_____

_____

_____

_____

_____

_____

_____

_____

_____

_____

_____

_____

_____

_____

_____

_____

_____

_____

Title: _____

Notes: _____

_____

_____

_____

_____

_____

_____

_____

_____

_____

_____

Title: _____

Notes: _____

_____

_____

_____

_____

_____

_____

_____

_____

_____

_____

_____

Title: _____

Notes: _____

_____

_____

_____

_____

_____

_____

_____

_____

_____

Title: _____

Notes: _____

_____

_____

_____

_____

_____

_____

_____

_____

_____

_____

Title: _____

Notes: _____

_____

_____

_____

_____

_____

_____

_____

_____

_____

Title: _____

Notes: _____

_____

_____

_____

_____

_____

_____

_____

_____

_____

_____

Title: _____

Notes:_____

_____

_____

_____

_____

_____

_____

_____

_____

_____

_____

_____

Title: _____

Notes: _____

_____

_____

_____

_____

_____

_____

_____

_____

_____

_____

_____

_____

_____

_____

_____

_____

_____

_____

_____

_____

_____

_____

_____

Title: _____

Notes:_____

_____

_____

_____

_____

_____

_____

_____

_____

_____

_____

Title:_____

Notes:_____

_____

_____

_____

_____

_____

_____

_____

_____

_____

_____

Title: _____

Notes: _____

_____

_____

_____

_____

_____

_____

_____

_____

_____

_____

_____

Title: _____

Notes: _____

_____

_____

_____

_____

_____

_____

_____

_____

_____

The JOURNEY to FREEDOM

The Journey With the Cross

An *Encounter* with God

Lesson 1
Understanding the Victory of the Cross
Your Power to Complete the Journey

Key Verse: *"I have been crucified with Christ; and it is no longer I who live, but Christ lives in me; and the life which I now live in the flesh I live by faith in the Son of God, who loved me and gave Himself up for me"* (Gal. 2:20 NASB).

Key Scriptures:
1 John 2:1–2; 4:4
1 Peter 2:24
2 Peter 1:3
1 Corinthians 1:18–23
2 Corinthians 8:9
Hebrews 12:1–3

Objective: The goal of this lesson is to teach you why you need the cross and what the cross has won for you.

Introduction: The Christian faith rests totally upon what Jesus Christ accomplished on the cross for all humanity. Without the victory won on the cross, the Christian would be totally helpless and powerless. Satan does not want you to comprehend the awesome victory of the cross. He wants you to live in unbelief and despair, ignorant of the Father's great love for you and desire to meet your needs.

God has established His promises and principles in the cross of Calvary. If God failed to sustain His people and meet them at every point of spiritual, physical, and material need, He would be denying the work He has already accomplished through His Son Jesus (2 Cor. 8:9). When you understand why you need the cross and when you are aware of the areas in which Christ triumphed on your behalf, you can begin the wonderful process of walking in victory in your daily Christian journey.

I.   There are five main reasons why you need the cross.

A.   You need the cross to free you from guilt and _____ (Ex. 34:7; Rom. 3:19).

1.   All of us stand guilty before a holy God. Our guilt before Him is of such a nature and extent that we could never atone for it ourselves. We need a perfect, sinless sacrifice to offer atonement for us.

2.   Jesus became our guilt-bearer. He bore our sins in His body on the tree (the cross).

B.   You need the cross to deliver you from the oppression of the _____ (Eph. 2:2; Heb. 2:14; Acts 10:38; Matt. 18:34).

1.   Ever since the Fall, all humankind has been separated from God. We have been oppressed by Satan and tormented by his attacks.

2. Jesus' death on the cross brought to an end the unchallenged power of Satan. He destroyed Satan's rule over the hearts and minds of people and brought freedom to all those oppressed by the devil.

C. You need the cross to heal you from _____ and suffering (Ps. 31:10).

1. Nowhere in the Bible do we read that sickness and suffering are the will of God. That is a common fallacy but is not supported by the Word of God.

2. Sin and sickness find their source in the work of Satan as the result of man's disobedience.

D. You need the cross to overcome anxiety and _____ (Gen. 3:17–19; 1 John 4:18).

1. After Adam and Eve sinned, humanity was sentenced to a life of hard labor (Gen. 3:17–19). Whereas Adam and Eve had lived in a garden full of God's bounty, surrounded by everything they needed for life and health, now they and all their descendants were condemned to a life of difficulty and effort.

2. Interestingly, thorns were part of the curse, and Jesus wore a crown of thorns when He was hanging on the cross. In this act, He took upon Himself all the agony of spirit and anxiety of heart that plague lost humanity apart from God.

3. What a contrast—the love of Jesus to the curse of thorns! Because He carried that curse for all of us, we are free, in the power of faith, to walk the way of God's kingdom (Matt. 6:33–34).

E.   You need the cross to defeat _____ (Rom. 6:23; Rev. 21:8).

1.   Because of sin, humanity was cut off from the source of life. Death is the result of our sin and is the common lot of all people (Rom. 5:12).

2.   The Bible tells us, however, that physical death is not the end, as we must face God's eternal judgment (Heb. 9:27–28).

3.   Through the death of Jesus, the judgment of death has been removed. He has borne the judgment for us (Heb. 2:14–15).

II.   There are four victories in the cross of Christ.

A.   The victory of _____ is in the cross (Rom. 5:1; Eph. 1:7; Col. 1:14).

1.   Christ has covered all your sins, and when you come to Him in repentance and confession, He never fails to cleanse you and give that sense of freedom and freshness which is your right through the death of the Savior (1 John 1:9).

2.   The devil does not want you to walk in Christ's forgiveness of sins. He loves to play on your feelings of weakness and tries to lead you back into condemnation and bondage. He bombards your mind with negative thoughts of unworthiness and false guilt.

3.   Satan tries to convince you that in some way you need to pay for your sins. However, this is a total contradiction to the teaching of Scripture and to the work of Calvary.

Jesus has paid for all your debt of sin, and you need only to receive your forgiveness in Him (Col. 2:13–15).

4.   As Savior, Jesus is at this very moment speaking to the Father on your behalf. As you open your mouth and ask for forgiveness, He is calling out your name before the heavenly Father (Heb. 7:25).

B.   The victory of _____ is in the cross (Rom. 8:32; 2 Cor. 8:9).

1.   The devil doesn't mind your believing in God, as long as He is a God who does nothing. Satan's aim is to destroy the trust in God that the Holy Spirit brought to life in your heart when you were born again.

2.   By the revelation of the Holy Spirit, you can know God as your Father and come to Him in simple trust and faith (Rom. 8:15–16). "He who did not spare his own Son, but gave him up for us all—how will he not also, along with him, graciously give us all things?" (Rom. 8:32).

3.   Every time you struggle with a sense of lack, you need only look to Calvary. Every other provision is only a footnote, since God has already given you Jesus, the greatest provision of all! All you ever need is included in Him, and through faith in Him, you experience the release of His provision into your life day by day.

C.   The victory of _____ over the devil is in the cross (Rom. 5:12, 15, 17; 1 John 3:8; Rev. 12:11).

1. When you have a clear understanding about your victory in Jesus, you will be able to overcome Satan in his attacks upon your life. In His death, Jesus triumphed over sin, death, the world, and the power of Satan.

2. Jesus has triumphed over sin and death (Rom. 5:12, 15). Through one man, Adam, sin and death entered the world, but through another man, Jesus, sin and death were unequivocally defeated.

3. Jesus has also triumphed over the world, that satanic system of evil that has permeated God's order and leads all men and women into darkness and away from God. Because of the finished work of Christ on the cross, you can share in His victory over the lure of the world (1 John 5:4–5).

4. Jesus has triumphed over Satan. That victory was not won in some dark and secret corner, but in a public arena for all to see. When Jesus cried out "It is finished," He was not crying out in weakness or despair, but proclaiming publicly the mighty victory of God. In Jesus, God has overcome all the powers of darkness so that they no longer pose a threat to those who stand in faith in Christ Jesus (Col. 2:13–16).

D.   The victory of _____ is in the cross (1 Pet. 2:24; Isa. 53:5; Ps. 103:3).

1. In the same way that the cross has the power to forgive your sins, it has the power to bring healing to your body. On His back, the Son of God purchased your healing. By His precious stripes, your physical healing was attained.

2.　　It is not the will of God that you live in sickness, just like it is not the will of God that you live in sin. On the cross, Jesus bought and paid for your healing. Sickness and disease no longer have authority over you; by Jesus' stripes, you are healed!

Summary: The cross of Christ is full of power. With it as an integral part of your faith, you can walk in victory over guilt and condemnation and over all the oppression of the devil. With the cross, you are a victor over sickness, suffering, anxiety, and fear. With the cross, you will even ultimately triumph over death. That's how powerful the cross is.

The cross has relevance in every area of your life. In the cross are forgiveness, freedom, provision, and healing. In the cross are found all the answers to life. The cross is the beginning and the end in your Christian journey.

Discussion Questions

1.　　Share your personal experience of your encounter at the cross.

2.　　In what area of your life do you need to claim the victory of the cross?

3.　　Share with one person why you need the work of the cross in your life.

Understanding the Victory of the Cross: Your Power to Complete the Journey

Scripture Memory for Week 1

"I have been crucified with Christ; and it is no longer I who live, but Christ lives in me; and the life which I now live in the flesh I live by faith in the Son of God, who loved me and gave Himself up for me" (Gal. 2:20 NASB).

Monday: Matthew 1:1–4:25 _____

_____

_____

Tuesday: Matthew 5:1–7:6 _____

_____

_____

Wednesday: Matthew 7:7–9:34 _____

_____

_____

Thursday: Matthew 9:35–12:14 _____

_____

_____

Friday: Matthew 12:15–13:52

_____

_____

Saturday: Matthew 13:53–16:12

_____

_____

Sunday: Matthew 16:13–19:12

_____

_____

Special Prayer Requests

_____

_____

_____

_____

Lesson 2
Establishing a Daily Time With God
Your Directions for the Journey

Key Verse: *"It happened that while Jesus was praying in a certain place, after He had finished, one of His disciples said to Him, 'Lord, teach us to pray just as John also taught his disciples' "* (Luke 11:1 NASB).

Key Scriptures:
Joshua 1:7–8
James 1:22–25
Exodus 34:29
Luke 5:16

Objective: In this lesson, you will learn why it is important to spend time with the Lord and how to implement this spiritual discipline into your life.

Introduction: In any relationship that is of value and that is going to grow and develop, communication is essential. So it is in your relationship with God. If you want to grow spiritually, you must devote time to talking to the Lord and learning how to listen as He speaks to you. In this way, you will build a relationship with the very source of life and truth, that is, God the Father, God the Son, and God the Holy Spirit.

I.   Why do you need a daily time with God?

A.   It will help you grow in _____ of God.

1.   A regular, systematic quiet time will help you to grow in understanding of God and His Word. It is one of the most basic disciplines you must learn as a new believer.

2.   The better you know Him and what He says in His Word, the better equipped you will be to serve Him. It has often been said that the Bible is God's love letter to you. How will you know His love for you unless you read His "letter"?

B.   It will help you develop a _____ relationship with God.

1.   Having regular fellowship with God is necessary if you really want to get to know Him in a personal way and have a living relationship with Him.

2.   You cannot have a relationship with anyone that you don't spend time with, and it's the same in your relationship with God.

C.   It will help you express your love and commitment to God.

1.   A regular quiet time is an expression of your love for God and commitment to Him and His ways.

2.   If you say you love Him but fail to spend time with Him, you would do well to examine your heart.

D.   It will help you receive _____ and guidance.

1.   During your quiet time, you can slow down enough to go before God and ask for the guidance you need in all areas of life.

2.   In particular, you can ask Him to be with you and direct your steps for that particular day. In that way, you will stay focused on His presence throughout all your daily activities.

E.   It will help you get equipped for the day.

1.   In the secret place of prayer, you can receive from God that which you need in order to do His will.

2.   In His presence, you draw strength, courage, and insight. Without His presence, you are left to your own feeble devices to manage your life.

F.   It will encourage your heart and renew your _____.

1.   Your spirit will be encouraged, renewed, and strengthened by a regular quiet time. It imparts strength for the day and refreshing for your heart.

2.   Having a quiet time will enable you to live as God desires, especially in the face of trials and temptations.

G.   It will cause you to grow in spiritual maturity.

1.   An effective, fruitful quiet time will help you to grow in spiritual maturity because you will be receiving spiritual food, or nourishment, from God.

2.   To neglect your quiet time is like neglecting to feed your physical body. In both instances, a lack of nourishment will weaken you and can even lead to death.

II.   There are two main parts of a quiet time with God.

A.   _____ is the first part.

1.   Prayer is a two-way communication with God. During prayer, you do set aside time to speak to Him, but you must also allow time for Him to speak to you.

2.   Most of us are much better at doing the speaking rather than the listening, so we all need to give special care to developing this part of our quiet time with the Lord.

B.   The _____ _____ _____ is the second part.

1.   God will speak to you through your Bible readings. His Word is "a lamp unto my feet, and a light unto my path" (Ps. 119:105 KJV).

2.   The Word of God will speak to your heart concerning actions, motives, and attitudes and will challenge you continually to grow in your relationship with God.

III. Here are two main suggestions for an effective quiet time.

A. **Choose a place that is _____.**

1. Your quiet time is your own special time to meet with God; therefore, you need to have no interruptions. Turn off the phone, the television, and the radio.

2. Remove yourself from the rest of your family. Find some private place in your home where you can be alone with God. (Some people have even used a closet!) Although you may occasionally pray with others, it is best to generally have your quiet time alone (Matt. 6:6; 14:23; Mark 1:35).

B. **Choose a definite _____.**

1. Usually, your days are very busy, so do not look for a break when it will be "convenient" to have your quiet time. Rather, build into your day a specific time to be with the Lord (Dan. 6:10).

   a. Find the time of day best-suited to your personal lifestyle. There are no hard and fast rules for the best time; however, it is generally recommended that you have your quiet time at the beginning of the day. This seems to work best for most people, since once the day is under way, it's hard to find the time.

   b. God deserves your best time, so set aside a certain amount of your prime time each day that is reserved for Him. Don't just squeeze in five minutes where you can. You need to give God ample time to speak to you.

2. Remember that the quality of your time with God is more important than the quantity. If you are faithfully spending a few minutes with the Lord each day, you will soon be increasing the time spent with Him as you mature in Christ. The key is consistency.

IV. Here are some more helpful prayer tips.

A.   Start your time of prayer with _____ and praise.

1. This is a good way to start your prayer time because it immediately causes you to acknowledge God's goodness and greatness. It takes the focus off you and puts it on God.

2. Consistently praising and thanking God for who He is and all He has done develops an "attitude of gratitude."

B.   _____ any sin or unforgiving attitude that the Holy Spirit brings to your attention.

1. Daily confession of sin is so vital to your relationship with God. If you never take the time to examine yourself, you'll never recognize those areas in which you are falling short.

2. The Holy Spirit will convict you of sin, if you ask Him. You don't have to try to analyze and dredge up every thought you ever had or everything you ever did; the Holy Spirit will bring to mind those things that are not pleasing to Him. At that point, confess it as sin, repent of it, and move on in your walk with God.

C.   Ask God for the things you need personally (Phil. 4:19; 2 Pet. 1:3; Matt. 6:33; 1 John 5:14–15).

1.   God cares about you and wants to provide for you. Making your needs known to God is an important part of your prayer time (but not the only part). Just like an earthly father wants to take care of his children, your heavenly Father wants to take care of you.

2.   Pray in faith, knowing that God hears you (James 1:5–7). Don't let yourself doubt His desire or ability to meet all your needs.

D.   _____ (stand in the gap) for others.

1.   You probably have unbelieving friends or relatives that need to come to the Lord. You probably also know many others with dire needs in their lives. In addition, your local church, your cell group, the government, and missionaries around the world need prayer.

2.   You won't pray for all these things every time you pray, but you should always take some time to pray for others. Be open for the guidance of the Holy Spirit as to which things you should pray for, and be specific in your requests on behalf of others.

E.   Always remember to _____ God for answered prayer.

1.   Remember to express your gratitude for specific answers to prayer. As you recall what He has done, faith will rise in your heart for future needs.

2. Some people like to keep a journal of prayer requests and then note the answers as they come. This is a wonderful way to keep track of what God is doing in your life and those you pray for.

F.   Leave time for God to speak to you personally.

1. Don't get so caught up in praying for your own needs or the needs of others that you neglect to leave time to hear from God. Nothing is as important as hearing personally from Him.

2. Sit quietly in the presence of the Lord and empty your mind of preconceived ideas as to what God should say. Wait, in a relaxed fashion, upon Him. Ask the Holy Spirit to speak to you, and respond when He does. You might sense an inward impression or you might become especially aware of His presence, but just allow Him to minister and speak in whatever way He chooses.

V.   Here are a few important final remarks.

A.   It is important to have a _____ quiet time.

1. You may find that you are naturally more drawn to either reading from the Word or praying. Both, however, are equally important.

2. Don't emphasize one over the other. As in all areas of life, balance is important, and the Holy Spirit will help you to find that balance.

B.   Be alert for opportunities to apply in your life what you are learning in your quiet time.

1.   Be a _____ of the Word, not a hearer only (James 1:22). Look for chances to apply the instructions you are receiving from the Word. Also, be ready to share with others what you are learning.

2.   Many times God will lead someone to you who needs the word that you received from the Lord that morning. Recognize the opportunity, and boldly share what God has given you.

C.   Stay in prayerful contact with God throughout the entire day (Luke 18:1).

1.   As you grow in Christ, prayer becomes woven into the fabric of your life. You develop a "prayerfulness" that enables you to immediately tap into God when needed.

2.   Your heart can be in a constant attitude of prayer, even when you are engaged in other activities. This is how you can fulfill the scriptural injunction to "pray without ceasing" (1 Thess. 5:17 KJV).

D.   Provide time during the week to allow deeper study of the _____ and more intensive _____.

1.   As you master the discipline of daily time with the Lord, you may find yourself yearning for even more in your quiet time with Him. That is a natural part of your spiritual growth. When you feast on a good meal, you generally want more, and when you begin partaking of the "deliciousness" of God's Word, you will want more of it.

2.   Set aside a block of undisturbed time where you can meet with God for an extended time of prayer. You might want to have one morning when you get up a little earlier, or you might want to set aside a special evening dedicated to prayer and Bible study. Be sensitive to the nudging of the Holy Spirit to lead you into special times of fellowship with Him.

Summary: The development of close, meaningful relationships is based on personal communication and shared activities. You will never get to really know God until you are spending time with Him on a regular, consistent basis. At first, it might seem like a task or duty to set aside time for prayer and Bible study, but as you begin this new discipline, it will soon evolve into a delightful part of your day. You will find yourself learning to hear His voice and experiencing His guidance and direction for your journey of faith.

Discussion Questions

1.   Have you started a regular daily time for reading God's Word and prayer? If not, what has prevented you from doing so? When will you begin?

2.   Do you communicate with God, and does He communicate with you? Be honest!

3.   What has God been saying to you, especially through His Word (the Bible)? Have you put it into practice?

4.   Do you know God better now than when you first became a disciple? Explain.

5.   When you have a quiet time, does it make a difference to your day? How? If not, why do you think that is so?

Establishing a Daily Time With God: Your Directions for the Journey

Scripture Memory for Week 2

"It happened that while Jesus was praying in a certain place, after He had finished, one of His disciples said to Him, 'Lord, teach us to pray just as John also taught his disciples' " (Luke 11:1 NASB).

Monday: Matthew 19:13–20:34 _____

_____

_____

Tuesday: Matthew 21:1–22:46 _____

_____

_____

Wednesday: Matthew 23:1–24:50 _____

_____

_____

Thursday: Matthew 25:1–26:75 _____

_____

_____

Friday: Matthew 27:1–28:20 _____

_____

_____

Saturday: Mark 1:1–2:28 _____

_____

_____

Sunday: Mark 3:1–4:41 _____

_____

_____

Special Prayer Requests _____

_____

_____

_____

_____

Lesson 3
Reading the Bible
Your Road Map for the Journey

Key Verses: *"But He answered and said, 'It is written, "Man shall not live by bread alone, but by every word that proceeds from the mouth of God" ' "* (Matt. 4:4 NKJV).

"Like newborn babies, long for the pure milk of the word, so that by it you may grow in respect to salvation" (1 Pet. 2:2 NASB).

Key Scriptures:
Psalm 1:1–3; 107:20; 119:9–11
Joshua 1:8
Proverbs 4:20–22
John 15:1–3
Isaiah 40:8
Matthew 24:35
James 1:23–25

Objective: The goal of this lesson is to help you understand why God's Word is a must for every person who claims Jesus Christ as Lord.

Introduction: A person cannot live without food and water, as both are required for healthy physical life. Spiritual life is no different; if you don't regularly feed from God's living bread of life, His Word, you will starve to death spiritually. Jesus said that man does not live by bread alone, but by every word that proceeds from God's mouth. When Jesus made this statement, He was being tempted by the devil. He successfully overcame the temptation, however, not by exerting pure willpower, but by exercising faith and trust in God's Word. As you feast daily from God's Word, you will find the nourishment you need on your journey of faith.

I.   Success for the journey comes through the Word of God.

A.   Living by the Word of God brings blessing (Ps. 1:1–3).

1.   The blessed man has abundant _____.

    a.   God desires for you to be prosperous in every area of your life. In 3 John 2 NKJV, the Word of God says, "Beloved, I pray that you may prosper in all things and be in health, even as your soul prospers."

    b.   The pathway to this life of blessing is found through the Word of God.

2.   The blessed man has _____.

    a.   WW. Wiersbe gives insight on the first part of verse 1 of Psalm 1. He says the phrase *blessed be the man* can be translated, "O the happiness of the man" (*Wiersbe's Expository Outlines on the Old Testament,* [Psalm 1:1], Victor Books, Wheaton, Illinois, 1993).

b.   No matter where you turn in the Bible, you'll find that God gives joy to the obedient, even in the midst of trial.

3.   The blessed man is _____ from the world (v. 1).

    a.   He "walks not in the counsel of the ungodly" (NKJV). Your Christian life is compared to a walk (Eph. 4:1, 17; 5:2, 8, 15). It begins with a step of faith in trusting Christ, and it grows as you take further steps of faith in obedience to His Word.

    b.   He does not "stand in the way of sinners."

    c.   Neither does the blessed man "sit in the seat of mockers."

    d.   If you start listening to the counsel (advice, plans) of the ungodly, you will soon be "standing" in their way of life, and finally you will "sit down" and agree with them.

4.   The blessed man is _____ with the Word of God (v. 2).

    a.   He not only reads the Word daily, but he also studies it, memorizes it, and meditates on it day and night. His mind is controlled by the Word of God; consequently, he is led by the Spirit and walks in the Spirit.

    b.   Meditation is to the soul what digestion is to the body. It includes contemplating the Word, "chewing on it" and applying it to your life, thus making it part of your inner person.

5.   The blessed man is situated by living _____ (v. 3).

    a.   Water for drinking is a picture of the Holy Spirit (John 7:37–39). In Psalm 1:3, the godly are compared to trees planted along a river that draw their sustenance from the life-giving flow of the water.

    b.   This world is a desert that can never satisfy your deepest needs. You must plant your spiritual roots deep into the things of Christ and draw upon the spiritual water of life.

    c.   Unless you spend time daily in prayer and the Word, allowing the Spirit to feed you, you will wither and die. If you draw upon the spiritual life found in the Word of God, however, you will be fruitful and successful in your faith.

B.   The Word of God brings true _____ (Josh. 1:3–8).

1.   God commissioned Joshua to achieve three things: lead the people into the land, defeat the enemy, and claim the inheritance.

2.   Since Joshua had a threefold task to perform, God gave him three special promises, one for each task. God promised to enable Joshua to cross the river and claim the land (vv. 3–4), defeat the enemy (v. 5), and apportion the land to each tribe as its inheritance (v. 6). God didn't give Joshua explanations as to *how* He would accomplish these things, because Joshua, like all God's people, had to live by faith in God's promises—not by logical explanations.

3.   The lesson for you as part of God's family is clear: God has given you "all spiritual blessings . . . in Christ" (Eph. 1:3 KJV), and you must step out by faith and claim them.

4. Joshua's strength and courage came from meditating on the Word of God, believing its promises, and obeying its precepts. Joshua had to take time to read it daily and make it a part of his inner person through meditation (Ps. 1:2; 119:97; see also Deut. 17:18–20).

5. The word *meditate* in the Hebrew is translated "to mutter." It was the practice of the Jews to read Scripture aloud (Acts 8:26–40) and talk about it to themselves and to one another (Deut. 6:6–9). This explains why God warned Joshua that the Book of the Law was not to depart out of his mouth (Josh. 1:8).

6. In your life as a Christian believer, prosperity and success aren't attained by following the standards of the world. These blessings are the by-products of your life when you are devoted to God and His Word.

C.   The Word of God brings _____ (Ps. 119:9–11).

1. Not only does God's Word promise to bless you and make you successful, it also promises to cleanse you.

    a. Just like you need to take a bath in order to get clean physically, you also need daily spiritual cleansing, and that comes from the Word of God.

    b. In Ephesians 5:26, the Bible says that Jesus cleanses the church by the washing of the Word. Jesus said in John 15:3 that you are clean by the word He speaks to you. Peter said that you escape the corruption that is in this world by God's great and precious promises (2 Pet. 1:4).

2.   Psalm 119:9 NASB asks a question then gives the answer: "How can a young man keep his way pure? By keeping it according to Your word."

    a.   Here the word *keeping* is referring to setting up a careful watch, like a security guard guarding a precious treasure.

    b.   The Word of God is like a security system over your heart, alerting you when the enemy is trying to get in.

3.   You must seek God with all your heart. You must diligently read and meditate daily on God's Word (2 Tim. 2:15).

4.   You also need to hide God's Word deep in your heart. It will prevent you from wandering away from Him and keep you in His blessing.

II.   Here are some tips for reading your Bible.

A.   Ask the Holy Spirit to be your _____, or counselor, so that you can learn the will and ways of God (John 16:13–14; Ps. 119:18).

1.   Be humble before the Lord and acknowledge your need for Him to reveal the truth of His Word to you. Don't think that you know it all or have heard it all before.

2.   The Holy Spirit knows the mind of God. When you ask for Him to enlighten your mind, He will quicken God's Word to your heart. Then you can more clearly and easily respond to His instructions.

B. _____ **what God is saying to you through the Bible (Heb. 3:7–8; 4:1–2), for faith comes by hearing the Word of God (Rom. 10:17).**

1. The Word of God is of no value to you unless you receive it in your heart and then act upon it in a corresponding manner. It has the power to change you from the inside out, if you will be teachable and quick to obey its commands.

2. The more you read God's Word, the more your faith will grow. The more your faith grows, the easier you will find it to obey Him. The more you obey Him, the more you will become like Him.

C. **Speak Scriptures out loud to God, to yourself, and to Satan.**

1. Use Scriptures in your words of praise to God and in praying to Him for needs. There is an inherent power that resides in them.

2. Speak Scriptures to yourself to feed your spirit, build your faith, and release divine purpose.

3. Declare Scripture to Satan to resist his attacks, just like Jesus did (Matt. 4:7). The Word of God is a powerful weapon that can demolish demonic strongholds.

D. _____ **on the Word (Prov. 4:20–23; Josh. 1:8).**

1. The words of Scripture are health and life to you. When you are constantly thinking on them, you are making yourself strong in your spirit.

2.   Study, prayer, and contemplation of the Word of God are not "extra" activities for superspiritual Christians. They are necessary for you and me, ordinary believers who want to know more about God and His ways.

E.   _____ to what you read in the Word by putting it into practice.

1.   James 1:23–24 says, "Anyone who listens to the word but does not do what it says is like a man who looks at his face in a mirror and, after looking at himself, goes away and immediately forgets what he looks like." In other words, such a person has no practical application of the Word of God in his life. His faith is nothing more than empty words.

2.   Verse 25 of James 1 continues by saying, "But the man who looks intently into the perfect law that gives freedom, and continues to do this, not forgetting what he has heard, but doing it—he will be blessed in what he does." Blessing awaits if you will put into practice those things you are learning from God's Word.

F.   Write down what God has impressed on your heart and mind through your Bible reading.

1.   Keeping a journal where you can jot down insights gained as you read God's Word is an excellent way to preserve His communication with you. If you do not record it, chances are that you will soon forget it!

2.   It is always faith-building and inspiring to look back some time later and see all that God has spoken to you and all the promises He has fulfilled.

G.   _____ verses from Scripture.

1. Most of us do not like to memorize, connecting it with school days that we would just as soon forget. But it is an extremely valuable tool for putting the Word of God in your heart where it can work to mature you.

2. Scripture memory is so important that we have included it in all the classes of the Journey as well as in the Discovery classes. Even when you have finished all the training, you should still be making Scripture memory a part of your devotional life.

Summary: The Bible provides your road map to your Christian journey. Without it, you will never reach your eternal destination of heaven. The more you know about the Bible, the stronger you will be in your faith and the less likely you will be to fall victim to Satan's attacks.

Listening to sermons, attending conferences, reading books, and watching Christian television are all good uses of time, but they are no substitute for the daily reading of God's Word. It is absolutely essential to your Christian growth. Make this discipline a part of your life and you'll soon be accelerating down the road of faith in your Christian journey.

Discussion Questions

1. Each day, write down one thing that God speaks to you from the Bible. Share with one other person what God reveals to you.

2. When do you have your daily time in the Word of God? What do you do during that time? In what ways would you like to improve your time in the Word?

3. Have you memorized a Bible verse that is particularly meaningful to you? If so, write it down from memory to the best of your ability.

Reading the Bible: Your Road Map for the Journey

Scripture Memory for Week 3

"But He answered and said, 'It is written, "Man shall not live by bread alone, but by every word that proceeds from the mouth of God" ' " (Matt. 4:4 NKJV).

Monday: Mark 5:1–6:56 _____

_____

_____

Tuesday: Mark 7:1–8:37 _____

_____

_____

Wednesday: Mark 9:1–10:52 _____

_____

_____

Thursday: Mark 11:1–12:44 _____

_____

_____

Friday: Mark 13:1–14:72 _____

_____

_____

Saturday: Mark 15:1–16:38 _____

_____

_____

Sunday: Luke 1:1–2:52 _____

_____

_____

Special Prayer Requests _____

_____

_____

_____

_____

Lesson 4
Knowing the Holy Spirit
Your Guide for the Journey

Key Verse: *"But when He, the Spirit of truth, comes, He will guide you into all the truth; for He will not speak on His own initiative, but whatever He hears, He will speak; and He will disclose to you what is to come"* (John 16:13 NASB).

Key Scriptures:
John 14:12, 15–27; 16:5–15
Acts 1:4–8
1 Corinthians 2:9–16

Objective: This lesson will help you understand who the Holy Spirit is and why He is so important.

Introduction: The Holy Spirit is not a vague influence or mystic idea—He is a person. This means He can communicate and make Himself real. You cannot necessarily see Him, but He is, nevertheless, always present.

The Holy Spirit is the third member of the threefold Godhead, and He is with you in every life situation. He reveals Jesus to you (John 15:26) and waits for you to respond to Him. He is a person, and He speaks to you personally.

Without the Holy Spirit, you could never live in the power of God or know God's strength in your daily life. He is the living water that sustains and refreshes (John 7:37–39). For abundance and fulfillment in life, you need this great gift of the Holy Spirit.

I.   The Bible describes the Holy Spirit.

A.   The Holy Spirit is given various names.

1.   He is the "good Spirit" (Neh. 9:20).

2.   He is "the Spirit of God" (Matt. 3:16).

3.   He is called the "_____" (John 14:16, 26 NIV).

4.   He is "the Spirit of truth" (John 16:13).

5.   He is referred to as "the Spirit of Christ" (Rom. 8:9).

6.   He is also called "the Spirit of sonship" (Rom. 8:15 NIV).

7.   He is "the Spirit of _____" (Heb. 10:29).

B.   The Holy Spirit is described through numerous symbols.

1.   He came as a _____ at Jesus' baptism (Matt. 3:16).

2. The Spirit spoke to Elijah through "a still small voice" (1 Kings 19:12–13 NKJV).

3. The terms *water* and *living water* are also used to describe Him (Isa. 44:3; John 7:37–39).

4. In the New Testament, the Holy Spirit came as a _____ upon the disciples gathered in the Upper Room (Acts 2:2).

5. The Holy Spirit came upon David when Samuel anointed him with oil (1 Sam. 16:13). Oil is often a symbol of the Holy Spirit.

6. The Holy Spirit made His presence known through visible flames of _____ (Acts 2:3).

II. The Holy Spirit is at work in you.

A. He empowers you to drive out _____ (Matt. 12:28; Mark 16:17)—You have supernatural authority over all the powers of darkness because of the Holy Spirit within you. This is how Jesus exercised His authority, and it is how you exercise yours. Casting out demons is one of the signs of a person who believes in Jesus. Have *you* cast out any demons lately?

B. He enables you to speak as God would have you speak (Mark 13:11)—You are not on your own to come up with the right thing to say in every circumstance you face. The Holy Spirit will give you the words to speak at the time you need them.

C. **He enables you to be born again (John 3:5–8)**—Salvation is a work of the Holy Spirit. He is the One who leads you to Jesus.

D. **He will be your Counselor _____ (John 14:16)**—The Holy Spirit will abide within you forever, as long as you desire Him and do not quench His work. He is always with you and will comfort, guide, and assist you in everything.

E. **He lives in you (John 14:17)**—The Holy Spirit actually resides within you. That means you do not have to reach up to heaven and pull Him down on your behalf; you only need to release His power that is already inside of you.

F. **He _____ you (John 14:26; 16:13–14)**—The Holy Spirit reveals the Word of God to you and teaches you all things. He speaks only what He hears from the Father and then imparts that to you. He always exalts Jesus.

G. **He gives you the power to be a witness (Acts 1:8)**—The ability to share Christ and the courage to proclaim Him come from the Holy Spirit. Just like He did for the disciples, He'll empower you to be a mighty, bold witness for Jesus.

H. **He causes God's _____ to be poured into your heart (Rom. 5:5)**—Where the Spirit of the Lord is, there is love. It is one of His defining marks. This selfless, agape love does not originate from you but comes from the Spirit's presence.

I.   **He helps you in your weakness (Rom. 8:26)**—When you do not know how to pray, the Spirit will intercede through you according to the perfect will of God. He can express what you cannot express, and through His intercession, you touch the heart of God.

J.   **He causes righteousness, peace, and joy to dwell in you (Rom. 14:17)**—These things will develop in you as you grow in the Lord.

K.   **He enables you to overflow with _____ (Rom. 15:13)**—The Holy Spirit can give you hope in the most hopeless situation and encouragement in the most discouraging trial. He gives you a heavenly perspective on every problem and difficulty.

L.   **He sanctifies you (Rom. 15:16)**—Sanctification, or growing in holiness, is a work of the Holy Spirit. It is an ongoing process that will never be fully completed in this world.

M.   **He gives you various gifts, as He determines (1 Cor. 12:4–11)**—The Holy Spirit imparts certain spiritual gifts to you that you might be a blessing to the body of Christ. He determines the dispensing of the gifts, not you. There is no one gift that is better than the others.

N.   **He enables the _____ of the Spirit to develop in you (Gal. 5:22–23)**—The fruit of the Spirit becomes evident in you as you walk daily with Him. As you learn to recognize His voice and respond to His direction, you slowly become transformed into the image of Christ.

III. There are four important reasons why you need the power of the Holy Spirit.

A.   **He gives you power to become God's _____.**

    1.   All of humanity has lost its way and does not recognize its true Father. Without the power of God at work, no one could ever become a child of God. The Holy Spirit's job is to awaken your sense of spiritual need and point you to Jesus, God's provision for humanity (John 1:12–13).

    2.   With the power of the Holy Spirit working in you, you can accomplish things that you could never do in your own strength. You can become God's child and live as a member of His family.

B.   **He gives you power for daily _____.**

    1.   The Holy Spirit gives you the power to live a daily life that is victorious and pleasing to Him.

    2.   God wants you to know His power so that you can live a life of faith that will be an example to others and point them to Christ.

C.   **He gives you power to overcome the _____.**

    1.   Every Christian believer lives in a war zone! Before you become a Christian, you are on Satan's side, but after you choose to follow Jesus, you join God's side (Eph. 2:1–5).

2. After you choose Christ, spiritual warfare and attack increase in your life. This is how Satan attempts to stop you from following Jesus. Through the power of the Holy Spirit within you, however, God makes His power available to give you strength and ability to defeat the devil (1 John 4:4).

D.   He gives you power to share and be a _____.

1. Acts 1:8 says, "You will receive *power* when the Holy Spirit comes on you; and you will be my witnesses in Jerusalem, and in all Judea and Samaria, and to the ends of the earth" (emphasis added).

2. In this verse, the Greek word for power is *dunamis,* which is the same word from which we derive the English word *dynamite.* God wants you to be filled with that same kind of power so you can be a witness for Him.

3. To be a witness means not only for you to speak about Jesus, but also for you to become like Jesus. In other words, when you speak, pray, and touch others in the power of the Holy Spirit, it is like Jesus Himself is present (John 14:12).

Summary: The Holy Spirit wants to have a relationship with you, just like the Father and Son do. He is a person—not a force. He is the one who leads you to salvation and causes you to grow in the Christian faith.

Cultivating a relationship with the Holy Spirit is exciting! He will use you as a vessel of healing, deliverance, and proclamation of the Gospel. He will develop the fruit of a sanctified life in you. He will transform you inside out as you cooperate with Him in making you a true disciple of Jesus.

Discussion Questions

1.   In what practical ways does the Holy Spirit help God's people to live as God intended?

2.   In what specific ways has the Holy Spirit helped you?

3.   Is your daily life an example to others of what it means to live as a true disciple of Jesus? If not, how could you improve?

4.   In what areas of your life do you need to yield to the Holy Spirit in order to be a more effective disciple of Christ?

Knowing the Holy Spirit: Your Guide for the Journey

Scripture Memory for Week 4

"But when He, the Spirit of truth, comes, He will guide you into all the truth; for He will not speak on His own initiative, but whatever He hears, He will speak; and He will disclose to you what is to come" (John 16:13 NASB).

Monday: Luke 3:1–4:44 _____

_____

_____

Tuesday: Luke 5:1–6:49 _____

_____

_____

Wednesday: Luke 7:1–8:56 _____

_____

_____

Thursday: Luke 9:1–10:42 _____

_____

_____

Friday: Luke 11:1–12:59 _____

_____

_____

Saturday: Luke 13:1–14:35 _____

_____

_____

Sunday: Luke 15:1–16:31 _____

_____

_____

Special Prayer Requests _____

_____

_____

_____

_____

Lesson 5
Conquering Temptation
Your Victory on the Journey

Key Verse: *"Be of sober spirit, be on the alert. Your adversary, the devil, prowls around like a roaring lion, seeking someone to devour. But resist him, firm in your faith, knowing that the same experiences of suffering are being accomplished by your brethren who are in the world"* (1 Pet. 5:8–9 NASB).

Key Scriptures:
1 Corinthians 10:13
Hebrews 2:18
James 1:12
2 Peter 2:9
2 Corinthians 2:11; 11:3
1 Thessalonians 3:5
Matthew 6:13
Luke 22:40

Objective: The goal of this lesson is to teach you how to overcome the trials and temptations of the devil.

Introduction: Ever since the beginning of time, Satan has had one chief goal: to separate men and women from the love and care of God the Father. To achieve this goal, Satan uses temptation to entice people to disobey God and fall into the bondage of sin and unbelief. This is what he did with Eve in the Garden of Eden (Gen. 3:1).

Satan is your enemy, and you must learn how to overcome his temptations. Although Satan is called the god of this world (2 Cor. 4:4), God has given you authority over him (Luke 10:19; Rom. 16:20). You can defeat him and reign victorious over him because of the authority won by Jesus' death on the cross.

Temptation is like a fishing lure. To the fish, the lure looks like food, apparently good and desirable. Satan uses the same technique on you. He uses three areas of temptation to try to lure you away from God: the lust of the flesh, the lust of the eyes, and the pride of life (1 John 2:15–17).

I.   There is a definite connection between worldliness and temptation.

A.   Worldliness is not so much a matter of *activity* as it is of _____.

1.   You can abstain from questionable amusements and doubtful places but still harbor a love for the world, for worldliness is a matter of the heart.

2.   The degree to which you love the world and the things in it is the degree to which you do not truly love the Father.

B.   Worldliness affects your response to God.

1.   Worldliness affects your response to the love of God.

a.   It will harden your heart to God's love at work in your life. It will cause you to not recognize His goodness at work on your behalf and His tender love that tries to draw you back to Him.

    b.   Doing the will of God is a joy for those living in the love of God. "If ye love Me, keep My commandments" (John 14:15 KJV). If you lose your enjoyment of the Father's love, you will find it hard to obey the Father's will.

    2.   Worldliness also affects your response to the will of God.

        a.   It causes you to be self-centered, wanting to pursue your own plans without considering God's plan for you.

        b.   "The world passeth away . . . but he that doeth the will of God abideth forever" (1 John 2:17 KJV). The world (Greek, *kosmos)* in this verse refers to an entity that is hostile to God. It is a seductive influence that you, like all Christians, must continually resist.

II.   There are three realms of temptation (1 John 2:15–17).

A.   The lust of the _____ is the first realm of temptation.

    1.   The flesh possesses appetites, desires, and attitudes that oppose the nature and character of the Holy Spirit (Gal. 5:19–24). The works of the flesh can be placed in one of the following three categories:

        a.   First are uncontrolled sexual appetites (v. 19).

        b.   Next are sins of rebellion and false religion (v. 20).

        c.   Then follow sins of hatred and envy (vv. 20, 21).

2.   You are to focus on developing the fruit of the Spirit in your life (Gal. 5:22–23).

3.   You are to put the flesh to death by the work of the cross of Christ (Gal. 5:24; Col. 3:5; 1 Pet. 2:11; 4:2).

4.   Satan tempted Jesus in this area of the flesh, but Jesus overcame him by standing firm on the Word of God and remaining faithful to God (Matt. 4:3–4).

B.   Next comes the lust of the _____.

1.   The lust of the eyes operates in a more subtle way and includes pleasures that gratify the sight and the mind.

   a.   In the days of the apostle John, the Greeks and Romans lived for entertainment and activities that excited the eyes. Times have not changed very much!

   b.   Regarding the dominance of television in our society, perhaps every Christian's prayer ought to be "Turn away my eyes from looking at vanity" (Ps. 119:37 NASB).

2.   Achan, a soldier, brought defeat to Joshua's army because of the lust of his eyes.

   a.   God had warned Israel not to take any spoils from the condemned city of Jericho, but Achan did not obey. He explained, "When I saw among the spoils a beautiful Babylonian garment, two hundred shekels of silver, and a wedge of gold weighing fifty shekels, I coveted them and took them" (Josh. 7:21a NKJV).

b.   The lust of the eyes led him into sin, and his sin caused the defeat of the entire army.

3.   David committed adultery with Bathsheba because he did not gain victory over his eyes.

    a.   He saw her and then he wanted her (2 Sam. 11:1–2). From that point on, he slid ever deeper into the quagmire of sin and finally ended up committing murder.

    b.   Remember: Sin will always take you further than you intended to go, keep you longer than you intended to stay, and cost you more than you intended to pay!

C.   Then there is the _____ of life.

1.   The third realm of temptation is the boastful pride of life.

    a.   God's glory is rich and full; man's glory is vain and empty. In 1 John 2:16, the Greek word for *pride* is the same word used to describe a braggart who tries to impress people with his importance.

    b.   People have always tried to outdo others in the way they live. The boastful pride of life motivates much of what such people do.

2.   The Bible is very clear when it warns against pride. Pride will bring you to shame (Prov. 11:2), and unchecked pride will eventually destroy you (Prov. 16:18).

3. The reason that love for the world is incompatible with love for God is that everything in the world is totally opposed to everything that God stands for. The pride of the world excludes God from its system of values and goals; thus, pride is the total opposite of the nature of Christ (Matt. 11:28–30).

4. It is easy to recognize when the pride of life, lust of the eyes, or lust of the flesh is influencing you.

    a. You will lose your enjoyment of the Father's love and lose your desire to do the Father's will.

    b. The Bible will become boring and prayer a difficult chore.

    c. Even Christian fellowship may seem empty and disappointing.

    d. When you see these things happening in your life, recognize that the devil is at work to lead you away from God.

III. You can overcome temptation (1 Cor. 10:13; 2 Pet. 2:9).

A.   Overcome temptation with _____.

1. Jesus said to pray that you would not be led into temptation (Luke 22:40).

2. Jesus taught that the prayer of forgiveness would deliver from temptation (Matt. 6:13–15).

B.   Overcome temptation with the Word of God.

1.   Every time Jesus was confronted with temptation, He answered with the Word of God (Matt. 4:1–11).

2.   The Word of God is a weapon that you can use to overcome the attacks of the enemy (Eph. 6:17).

C.   Overcome temptation with the _____ of the Lamb.

1.   "And they overcame him by the blood of the Lamb and the word of their testimony" (Rev. 12:11 NKJV).

2.   Proclaiming the power of the blood of Christ in your life releases supernatural force on your behalf. Nothing is more powerful than the precious blood of the Lamb that paid for your redemption.

D.   Overcome temptation by _____ with strong believers.

1.   You must "flee the evil desires of youth and pursue righteousness, faith, love and peace, along with those who call on the Lord out of a pure heart" (2 Tim. 2:22; see also 1 Tim. 6:11).

2.   Remember that bad company will corrupt good morals (1 Cor. 15:33). You cannot be in partnership with unbelievers who don't want to serve God (2 Cor. 6:14–18).

Summary: Temptation is a part of life that you cannot escape from. The fact that you are tempted to sin does not mean that you are backslidden. It only means that you, like all people, still reside in a fallen world of sin and temptation.

You do not have to live as a victim of constant temptation, forever succumbing to things you really don't want to do. Prayer, the Word of God, and fellowship with other Christians will help you grow strong and be able to resist temptation. Because of Jesus' death and resurrection, Satan has already been defeated, and as a child of God, you can appropriate that victory in every temptation that assaults you.

Discussion Questions

1. What temptations are you facing right now that are troubling you? Ask your team leader to share Scriptures with you that will help you overcome.

2. What are some effective ways to overcome temptation?

3. What is the lust of the flesh? Do you struggle in this area?

4. What is the lust of the eyes? Why is it so prevalent?

5. What is the pride of life? Why is its influence so difficult to detect?

Conquering Temptation: Your Victory on the Journey

Scripture Memory for Week 5

"Be of sober spirit, be on the alert. Your adversary, the devil, prowls around like a roaring lion, seeking someone to devour. But resist him, firm in your faith, knowing that the same experiences of suffering are being accomplished by your brethren who are in the world" (1 Pet. 5:8–9 NASB).

Monday: Luke 17:1–18:43 _____

_____

_____

Tuesday: Luke 19:1–20:47 _____

_____

_____

Wednesday: Luke 21:1–22:71 _____

_____

_____

Thursday: Luke 23:1–24:53 _____

_____

_____

Friday: John 1:1–2:25 _____

_____

_____

Saturday: John 3:1–4:54 _____

_____

_____

Sunday: John 5:1–6:71 _____

_____

_____

Special Prayer Requests _____

_____

_____

_____

_____

Lesson 6
Becoming a Part of the Church Family
Your Connection With Others on the Journey

Key Verses: *"Day by day continuing with one mind in the temple, and breaking bread from house to house, they were taking their meals together with gladness and sincerity of heart"* (Acts 2:46 NASB).

"This is My commandment, that you love one another, just as I have loved you. Greater love has no one than this, that one lay down his life for his friends" (John 15:12–15 NASB).

Key Scriptures:
1 Corinthians 12:25–27; 13:1–8
Romans 12:9–21
Philippians 2:1–4
Acts 4:32–35
1 John 1:7; 3:16–18; 4:20–21
John 13:35
Ephesians 4:13–16, 25
1 Thessalonians 5:12–15

Objective: In this lesson, you will learn the value of being connected to the local church family.

Introduction: John Wesley once said, "The Bible knows nothing of solitary religion." Christianity is a religion of fellowship. Following Christ means living in love, righteousness, and service, and these things can be achieved only through the social relationships found in the church. Nothing can take the place of being a part of the local church.

Satan will try to convince you that you do not need to be concerned about other people. He will tell you that as long as you have God, you don't need other Christians. However, the truth is, you are one of the living stones that God is using to build a spiritual house (1 Pet. 2:5; Eph. 2:20–22). The house would be incomplete without you. You need other Christians, and they need you.

The word *fellowship* in Greek is the word *koinonia,* and it means "communion," or "sharing in common" (see Acts 2:42; 1 John 1:7). This word describes how Christians should live; that is, as a community of people who share the selfless, sacrificial agape love of God (Rom. 5:5; John 13:34; 1 John 3:23).

I.   Christians possess a _____ of the Spirit.

A.   The fellowship of the Spirit is an attitude of heart and mind.

1. It is the expression of a bond in Christ Jesus between Christian believers that goes even deeper than the natural ties of family or friendship.

2. One of the greatest challenges to your life as a Christian is to walk in this fellowship of the Spirit.

B.   **As a Christian, you are not _____.**

     1.   Many Christians often give up in their service for the Lord because they feel that they are on their own and no one really cares for them. They feel that the problems they are facing are peculiar to themselves alone.

     2.   By faith, you have been born into a tremendous worldwide family of believers joined together, not by race, color, or convenience, but by the blood of Jesus (Gal. 3:26–28). You are not a spiritual orphan, but part of a wonderful family.

II.   The fellowship of the Spirit provides many blessings.

A.   **The Holy Spirit brings love (Rom. 15:30).**

     1.   The love of the Spirit is at the heart of your relationships with other believers. This is not a love that grows out of natural affection, but it is rather a love produced within you by the direct work of the Holy Spirit (Rom. 5:5).

     2.   Jesus said the reality of this love would be the hallmark of Christian discipleship to the world (John 13:35).

B.   **The Holy Spirit brings _____ (Gal. 3:26–28).**

     1.   Your unity with other Christians is based on your shared faith in Christ and the common bond of the Holy Spirit (1 Cor. 12:13). Along with other Christians, you enjoy access to the Father through the Holy Spirit (Eph. 2:17–18).

2.   This unity of the Spirit is precious and needs to be guarded and persevered in (Eph. 4:3).

C.   The Holy Spirit makes you part of the _____ of the Lord (Eph. 2:21–22).

1.   Christians are joined together as a holy temple in which God lives by His Spirit. This temple, or house of God, is also the place of service, offering, and praise (1 Pet. 2:5).

2.   God regards this building as very significant; thus, you must be very careful of how you build on the foundation already laid (1 Cor. 3:10–17).

3.   It is no light thing to play around with the temple of God, because you will be held accountable before Him as to what you do with His precious dwelling place.

D.   The Holy Spirit gives gifts to the body of Christ (1 Cor. 12:7–11).

1.   Although the gifts of the Holy Spirit are manifested through individual believers, they are, in fact, gifts to the body. Gifts of the Spirit are not meant for your own personal pleasure or whim. They edify the body.

2.   The gifts of the Holy Spirit make no sense apart from the fact of the fellowship of the Spirit. Their operation should be a sign of the unity of the body.

E.   The Holy Spirit causes you to _____ (John 4:23–24).

1.   "God is Spirit, and those who worship Him must worship in spirit and truth" (v. 24 NKJV).

2.   Christian fellowship is most deeply expressed in worship, and true worship finds its root in the work of the Holy Spirit (Phil. 3:3).

III. Christian fellowship brings three specific results.

A.   **Fellowship brings _____.**

1.   The psalmist in Psalm 133 says that unity is like the dew of Hermon falling on Mount Zion. The dew of Hermon is the source of water and life for the land, bringing refreshment and sustenance and enabling the people to produce their crops.

2.   Fellowship does the same for you in that it brings refreshment and nourishment to your soul, enabling you to be spiritually fruitful.

B.   **Fellowship provides spiritual _____.**

1.   There are many areas in your Christian life where you cannot function properly without fellowship with other believers. In the end, Christian fellowship is not an individual exercise, but a corporate one.

2.   The Holy Spirit moves to bring unity in the body of Christ, and He gives gifts as they are needed to build up and keep the body whole. There should be no poverty of spirit or lack of spiritual gift in the body, and everyone should be enriched and built up as spiritual gifts are shared in mutual love and service (1 Pet. 4:10–11).

3.   The Father's will is that Christians walk in a generosity of spirit that recognizes what is of God in one another and fosters it through mutual encouragement and help (Heb. 10:24–25).

C.   Fellowship provides _____.

1.   Responsible parents do not abandon their children. They make sure to care and provide for them. God is your heavenly Father, and He cares for you and each person who comes to Him.

2.   God shows His love for you by putting you into the safety of a loving and caring family of believers that can help you grow to spiritual maturity.

   a.   Within the local church congregation, you receive pastoral oversight from the senior pastor and staff pastors. "Their work is to watch over your souls, and they know they are accountable to God" (Heb. 13:17 NLT).

   b.   In addition to receiving pastoral oversight, we place you in a small group that meets weekly in a home. In that group, you receive the individual care and attention that you need to grow into an effective disciple of God.

3.   "This is how we know what love is: Jesus Christ laid down His life for us. And we ought to lay down our lives for our brothers. . . . Dear children, let us not love with words or tongue but with actions and in truth" (1 John 3:16, 18).

IV.   Christians need to keep right attitudes towards others in the body of Christ.

A. Christians should:

1. Love one another (John 13:34–35; 15:12, 17; 1 Thess. 3:12; 4:9; 1 Pet. 1:22; 1 John 3:18; 4:7, 11–12).

2. Encourage one another (1 Thess. 4:18; Heb. 3:13; 10:25).

3. _____ one another (Rom. 14:19).

4. Admonish one another (Col. 3:16).

5. Serve one another (Gal. 5:13; 1 Pet. 4:10).

6. Bear with one another (Eph. 4:2; Col. 3:13).

7. Forgive one another (Eph. 4:32; Col. 3:13).

8. Be _____ to one another (Eph. 4:32).

9. Be compassionate to one another (Eph. 4:32; 1 Pet. 3:8).

10. Accept one another (Rom. 15:7).

11. Pray for one another (James 5:16).

12. Carry one another's _____ (Gal. 6:2).

B.   Christians should not:

1.   Bite or devour one another (Gal. 5:15).

2.   Provoke or _____ one another (Gal. 5:26).

3.   Hate one another (Titus 3:3).

4.   _____ one another (Rom. 14:13).

5.   Lie to one another (Col. 3:9).

6.   _____ or speak evil about one another (James 4:11).

Summary: The English poet John Donne said, "No man is an island," and that is particularly true in the body of Christ. When you are born again, you become part of a spiritual family that is just as real as your natural family. To isolate yourself from your Christian brothers and sisters is to isolate yourself from the expression of Christ on the earth.

Participation in Christian fellowship through a local church body yields many benefits. You will grow in love, unity, and spiritual maturity. You will be equipped, protected, and encouraged so that you can become fruitful in God's kingdom. In short, you will become all that you can be only as you stay connected to the corporate body of Christ.

Discussion Questions

1. Why do you need other Christians for your spiritual growth? Share how someone else has helped you grow in your faith.

2. Are home groups a valid biblical part of church life? (See Acts 2:42–47; 4:32–35; 12:12; 16:40; Col. 4:15; Philem. 2.) How has your small group helped you grow in your faith?

3. Did Jesus have close friends? (See Mark 5:37; Luke 9:1; 10:1; John 20:2; Acts 1:15.) What was Jesus' attitude towards Christian unity? (See John 17:20–23.)

4. Make a list of practical ways in which you can express your commitment to others by serving. (See Phil. 2:4.) Ask the Lord to fill you with His love so that you will be eager to serve others, knowing that you are truly serving Christ Jesus. (See Matt. 25:31–46.)

Becoming a Part of the Church Family: Your Connection With Others on the Journey

Scripture Memory for Week 6

"Day by day continuing with one mind in the temple, and breaking bread from house to house, they were taking their meals together with gladness and sincerity of heart" (Acts 2:46 NASB).

Monday: John 7:1–8:53 _____

_____

_____

Tuesday: John 9:1–10:42 _____

_____

_____

Wednesday: John 11:1–12:50 _____

_____

_____

Thursday: John 13:1–14:31 _____

_____

_____

Friday: John 15:1–16:33 _____

_____

_____

Saturday: John 17:1–18:40 _____

_____

_____

Sunday: John 19:1–21:25 _____

_____

_____

Special Prayer Requests _____

_____

_____

_____

_____

Lesson 7
Sharing Your Faith
Your Invitation to Others to Join the Journey

Key Verse: *"One of the two who heard John speak and followed Him, was Andrew, Simon Peter's brother. He found first his own brother Simon and said to him, 'We have found the Messiah' (which is translated, the Christ). . . . Philip found Nathanael and said to him, 'We have found Him of whom Moses in the Law and also the Prophets wrote—Jesus of Nazareth, the son of Joseph' "* (John 1:40–41, 45 NKJV).

Key Scriptures:
John 14:12; 15:16
Acts 4:29–31
Isaiah 55:11
Ephesians 2:10
Philippians 2:10–11
Romans 10:14–15
2 Corinthians 6:1

Objective: In this lesson, you will learn the importance of telling others about Jesus and will learn how to pray for others to come to Christ.

Introduction: The Greek word for *salvation* could be translated "safety," or "soundness." When you were born again and became a child of God, you were made whole, or safe and sound. Therefore, when you speak to others about the salvation available in Jesus, you are revealing to them how they, too, can become whole and safe. There are two aspects to this view of salvation: reconciliation to God, which is made possible through Jesus' death, and regeneration to new life, which is made possible because of Jesus' resurrection.

You do not need to wait until you are perfect before you can make disciples for Jesus. You must get on with the job of fulfilling the Great Commission, while at the same time allowing God to continue making all the adjustments that are necessary in your life. You must not permit laziness, complacency, unbelief, or lack of love to stop you from doing what Jesus has asked all His disciples to do: to win souls and make disciples.

I. There are three main forces that will enable you to make disciples.

A. The _____ of Jesus Christ will compel you to share your faith.

1. In 2 Corinthians 5:14, the Bible says, "For the love of Christ *compels* us. . . ." (emphasis added). The word *compel* is a forceful word, implying strength and power. It indicates a compulsion beyond your natural self, so great is its power.

2. When this type of love is burning in your heart, you yearn for everyone else to share in the wonderful experience of Christ and His love. You can hardly stand to keep the Good News to yourself.

B. The _____ of God will enable you to share your faith.

1. "But you shall receive power when the Holy Spirit has come upon you; and you shall be witnesses to Me in Jerusalem, and in all Judea and Samaria, and to the end of the earth" (Acts 1:8 NKJV).

2.   One of the most wonderful things the Holy Spirit does is give you power to be a witness for Him. Apart from the Spirit, you can do nothing; full of the Spirit, you become a bold witness of what Christ has done for you and what He can do for others.

C.   **The _____ of God will propel you into sharing your faith.**

1.   "Since, then, we know what it is to fear the Lord, we try to persuade men" (2 Cor. 5:11).

2.   A healthy, reverential respect for God and humble awareness of His omnipotence will cause you to want to share Him with others. When you know their eternal destiny apart from Christ, the fear of the Lord on their behalf will propel you to action.

II.   Prepare yourself to be a witness.

A.   **Be filled with the Holy Spirit.**

1.   Ask the Holy Spirit to fill you and anoint you to lift up Jesus Christ, and to empower you for His service.

2.   Ask daily for the Spirit's infilling; it is not a one-time event. Then you will always be ready to give a clear witness of the hope of Christ within you.

B.   **_____ to the Holy Spirit.**

1.   Surrender yourself to the control of the Holy Spirit. Actually tell Him you are giving Him your body, mind, will, and emotions so that He might use you as His obedient vessel.

2.   You will still make your own decisions, but you will also be guided and influenced as to what to do and say. This is the essence of the Spirit-filled life.

C.   Be a _____.

1.   Ask the Holy Spirit to flow out from you to touch other people's lives and to minister through you to other people.

2.   In John 7:37–39, Jesus spoke of the Spirit as living water. You are simply a channel filled with the life-giving water of the Spirit, ready to be released into the lives of others.

D.   Speak His Word.

1.   Ask the Holy Spirit to put His words in your mouth; that is, to bring to mind something from Scripture or to give you any word or vision necessary for whatever situation you face.

2.   Ask Him to anoint your lips to speak in the way that He desires. Ask Him to give you words of power, authority, challenge, conviction, life, liberty, love, and compassion.

E.   Be _____.

1.   Thank the Lord for answering your prayers to be a witness and to be full of His Spirit. This will make you more conscious of His presence within you.

2.   A grateful heart builds faith, and when you believe He has heard you, you'll find it easier to believe He'll use you to minister to others.

F.   Get to know Jesus better.

1.   "That I may know Him" (Phil. 3:10 NKJV) expresses the cry of every heart truly following after God. The more you know Him, the more you will be able to commit yourself to Him and the more you will be able to share confidently with others.

2.   You can get to know Jesus better through reading God's Word, praying, and fellowshipping with other Christians.

G.   Follow Jesus more closely.

1.   Jesus' call to you is the same call He made to His disciples: "Follow Me, and I will make you fishers of men" (Matt. 4:19 NKJV).

2.   The only way to follow Jesus is to follow His example and do what God asks you to do day by day. First you follow Him, and then He uses you to bring others into His kingdom.

H.   _____ _____ Jesus with your life, actions, and words.

1.   Your fine words or persuasiveness will not draw people to Jesus, but lifting Him up and exalting Him clearly before them will (John 12:32).

2.   Your life is your most powerful tool in influencing friends, relatives, and other people and in leading them to Jesus. It has often been said that your life may be the only Bible some people will ever read.

3.   How can people tell whether you have Christ in you and are filled with the Holy Spirit?

      a.   Consider this example: Think of yourself as an unmarked tube. When you are squeezed by the pressures of life, what comes out? Is it impatience, tension, anger, and frustration, or is it love, joy, peace, and patience?

      b.   Others will look to see what comes out of your life, particularly when you face difficulty, because they will want to know if you live what you preach.

III. Take time to pray for the lost.

A.   Ask God to _____ them to Himself (John 6:44)—Lost people cannot make themselves want to get saved. God must draw them to Him.

B.   Pray that they will seek to know God (Acts 17:27; Deut. 4:29)—Ask God to cause them to hunger after Him and to have a desire for Him.

C.   Pray that they will believe the Scriptures (1 Thess. 2:13; Rom. 10:17)—Truth is in the Scriptures, so pray that they will accept the standard of the Word of God. It has the power to save.

D.   _____ Satan from blinding them to the truth (Matt. 13:19; 2 Cor. 4:4)—Satan seeks to keep the lost deceived, blinded, and bound. Actively resist his work in their lives.

E.   Pray for the Holy Spirit to work in them (John 16:8–13)—Release the Holy Spirit to convict them of sin and to reveal to them truth. That is His role, not yours.

F.   Ask God to send someone to lead them to Christ (Matt. 9:37–38)—Ask the Father for handpicked laborers that can especially minister to your loved ones in their particular circumstances.

G.   Pray that they will believe in Christ as _____ (John 1:12; 5:24)—They must believe in Jesus' saving, atoning work. It is not enough to acknowledge Him as a teacher or prophet.

H.   Pray that they will turn from sin (Acts 17:30–31)—Ask God to grant them true repentance—not worldly sorrow—that will enable them to forsake sin.

I.   Pray that they will confess Christ as _____ (Rom. 10:9–10)—This is your ultimate goal for them: that they would receive Jesus Christ as their personal Lord and Savior.

J.   Pray that they will yield all to follow Christ (2 Cor. 5:15; Phil. 3:7–8)—Pray that they will have a heavenly perspective and will not be entrapped by worldly pleasures and desires.

K.   Pray that they will take _____ and grow in Christ (Col. 2:6–7)—Pray not only for them to come to Christ, but also that their salvation would be real, stable, and permanent.

IV. Live as a true child of God.

A. Be _____ and sincere in your life with God.

1. Do not be a callous, thoughtless fanatic. Be natural about your Christianity. The joy of Christ speaks for itself.

2. Jesus said you are to be the salt of the earth (Matt. 5:13–16). Be salt, wherever you go!

    a. Salt purifies, heals, preserves, and disinfects. Therefore, because of Christ in you, you render a tremendous effect wherever you go, without even realizing it.

    b. Another thing that salt does is to make people thirsty. Your life should make people thirsty for the life of Christ.

B. As you live genuinely as a disciple of Jesus, you will attract people to Christ.

1. Remember: A witness is not called to be judge, defense attorney, or prosecutor. A witness is simply called to give the facts, as he knows them.

2. Let God do the convicting and judging; you just share what you know to be true in your life.

Summary: Sharing your faith is a natural outgrowth of life in your Christian journey. It is normal to want others to know and experience what you have found in Christ. Sharing Christ is motivated by the love of God for the lost and is accomplished through the power of the Holy Spirit.

The best way to share Christ is to live your life in such a way that His lordship is easily recognizable. When others can see Christ in you, they will want to know what makes you so different and how they can have what you have. Then the words you share will reinforce what you have already lived before them.

You do not have to be perfect in order for God to use you in sharing your faith. You only need to be willing and obedient to the leading of the Holy Spirit. He will lead you to those who are waiting for someone to invite them to join the journey of following Jesus. Why not be the one?

Discussion Questions

1. What happens in heaven whenever anyone is saved? (See Luke 15:5–7, 22–24, 32.)

2. How do the love of God, fear of God, and power of God motivate Christians to witness?

3. Ask God to show you any blockages that are preventing you from becoming a fisher of men. Pray for one another for the removal of these hindrances.

4. Fear is the most common factor that hinders witnessing. What does the Word of God say about fear of man? (See 2 Tim. 1:7; 1 Pet. 3:13–16.)

5. Begin praying and looking in faith for those you can bring to the Lord and those whom you can disciple.

Sharing Your Faith: Your Invitation to Others to Join the Journey

Scripture Memory for Week 7

"One of the two who heard John speak and followed Him, was Andrew, Simon Peter's brother. He found first his own brother Simon and said to him, 'We have found the Messiah' (which is translated, the Christ). . . . Philip found Nathanael and said to him, 'We have found Him of whom Moses in the Law and also the Prophets wrote—Jesus of Nazareth, the son of Joseph'" (John 1:40–41, 45 NKJV).

Monday: Psalm 1 _____

_____

_____

Tuesday: Psalm 2 _____

_____

_____

Wednesday: Psalm 3 _____

_____

_____

Thursday: Psalm 4 _____

_____

_____

Friday: Psalm 5 _____

_____

_____

Saturday: Psalm 6 _____

_____

_____

Sunday: Psalm 7 _____

_____

_____

Special Prayer Requests _____

_____

_____

_____

_____

Continuing the Journey . . .

Congratulations! You have just completed ninety days of change! You have committed your life to Christ, encountered Him face to face, and learned the basics of following Him for the rest of your life. Your journey has probably been full of surprises and adventures, and unexpected twists and turns. That's like any journey you take. But your eternal destination for this earthly journey is heaven, and when you get there one day, the earthly journey will seem brief and inconsequential compared to the glory revealed.

These ninety days of change have launched you on a journey that will last a lifetime. You have not learned it all just because you've finished this first part of your journey. No, growing and learning are continual processes, and there is so much more the Lord wants you to discover about Him.

To that end, we encourage you to join us for the next phase of your Christian journey: a series of classes called "Discovery." We have three levels of classes, each composed of ten weeks. During these thirty weeks, you'll discover biblical principles and direction that will help you mature in Christ. You'll learn much more to strengthen you in your walk with Christ, and you'll also discover the joy of seeing God use you to minister to others. These Discovery classes will take you further in your journey, so we hope you'll join us. The "Journey" may have ended, but the "Discovery" is just beginning!

Answer Key

The Journey With the Cross

Lesson 1

Page 68
Condemnation
Devil

Page 69
Pain
Fear

Page 70
Death
Forgiveness

Page 71
Provision
Triumph

Page 72
Healing

Lesson 2

Page 78
Knowledge
Living

Page 79
Direction
Spirit

Page 80
Prayer
Word of God

Page 81
Quiet
Time

Page 82
Thanksgiving
Confess

Page 83
Intercede
Thank

Page 84
Balanced

Page 85
Doer
Word, prayer

Lesson 3

Page 90
Life
Joy

Page 91
Separated
Saturated

Page 92
Water
Success

Page 93
Cleansing

Page 94
Teacher

Page 95
Accept
Meditate

Page 96
Respond
Memorize

Lesson 4

Page 102
Counselor
Grace
Dove

Page 103
Wind
Fire
Demons

Page 104
Forever
Teaches
Love

Page 105
Hope
Fruit

Page 106
Child
Living
Devil

Page 107
Witness

Lesson 5

Page 112
Attitude

Page 113
Flesh

Page 114
Eyes

Page 115
Pride

Page 116
Prayer

Page 117
Blood
Fellowshipping

Lesson 6

Page 122
Fellowship

Page 123
Alone
Unity

Page 124
Temple
Worship

Page 125
Fruitfulness
Equipping

Page 126
Safety

Page 127
Edify
Kind
Burdens

Page 128
Envy
Judge
Slander

Lesson 7

Page 134
Love
Power

Page 135
Fear
Yield

Page 136
Channel
Thankful

Page 137
Lift up

Page 138
Draw
Bind

Page 139
Savior
Lord
Root

Page 140
Genuine